Pebble® Plus

Canadian Symbols

Totem Poles

by Sabrina Crewe

CAPSTONE PRESS
a capstone imprint

Pebble Plus is published by Capstone Press,
1710 Roe Crest Drive, North Mankato, Minnesota 56003
www.capstonepub.com

Library of Congress Cataloging-in-Publication Data
Cataloging-in-publication information is on file with the Library of Congress.

ISBN 978–1-4914-7092-3 (library binding : alk. paper)
ISBN 978–1-4914-7098-5 (pbk. : alk. paper)
ISBN 978–1-4914-7110-4 (eBook PDF)

Developed and Produced by Discovery Books Limited
Paul Humphrey: project manager
Sabrina Crewe: editor
Ian Winton: designer

Photo Credits
Regien Paassen/Shutterstock: cover; Andrea Izzotti/Shutterstock: title page; Meunierd/Shutterstock: 5; Bill Perry/Shutterstock: 7; Fotocraft/Shutterstock: 9 (main image); Chris Cheadle/Alamy: 9 (inset top); Matabum/Shutterstock: 9 (inset bottom); Gunter Marx/Alamy: 11, 19; 2009fotofriends/Shutterstock: 13 (left); Kirsten Wahlquist/Shutterstock: 13 (right); Riekephotos/Shutterstock: 15; JosefHanus/Shutterstock: 17; Cliff LeSergent/Alamy: 21.

Note to Parents and Teachers
This book describes and illustrates totem poles. The images support early readers in understanding text. The repetition of words and phrases helps early readers learn new words. This book also introduces early readers to subject-specific vocabulary words, which are defined in the Glossary section. Early readers may need assistance to read some words and to use the Table of Contents, Glossary, Read More, Internet Sites, and Index sections of the book.

Printed in China through World Print Ltd in 2014
007272WPS15

Table of Contents

A Symbol for Canada

A symbol is a picture or thing that stands for something important. Some First Peoples carve totem poles with their important symbols. Today, the totem pole is a symbol for Canada, too.

This totem pole is outside a government building.

Making Totem Poles

The western coast of Canada had plenty of food for First Peoples. They fished and found fruits and nuts. Because it was easy to find food, the people had time to make totem poles.

Canada's first totem poles were made on the western coast.

Most totem poles are made from cedar trees. Cedar wood is good for carving and lasts a long time. Many totem poles are painted with bright colours after they are carved.

A tall red cedar tree

Carving a totem pole

Part of a painted totem pole

9

Clans and Symbols

Clans are groups within a nation. Clan members share the same stories. First Peoples carved their clan symbols on totem poles. "Totem" comes from an Ojibway word for family symbol.

These members of the Nisga'a Nation are celebrating a new totem pole.

Clans often have animals as their symbols. First Peoples carve many animals into their totem poles. You may see bears, wolves, fish, frogs, and birds.

Some First People clans have the sea otter as their symbol.

Telling Stories

If you understand the symbols, you can read the totem pole's story. The thunderbird is one of the best-known symbols on totem poles. It is not a real bird, but it appears in many legends.

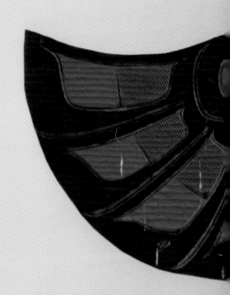

A thunderbird has huge wings for making thunder.

15

Totem poles can tell the story of a real event. They are also used to honour ancestors and celebrate clan members. Totem poles sometimes support buildings and form doorways.

This totem pole is also a doorway.

Tall Totem Poles

When a totem pole is finished, it must be raised. The raising ceremony happens at a potlatch. The potlatch is a big feast. It takes many people to raise a tall totem pole.

Raising a Nisga'a totem pole

Most totem poles are between 3 and 20 metres high. Some of them are even taller. Many of the world's tallest totem poles are in British Columbia.

This totem pole in Alert Bay, B.C., is more than 50 metres tall!

Glossary

ancestor—a person in your family or clan who came before you

carve—to cut shapes into wood

clan—a connected group of people, like a family but larger

nation—a country or a large group of people with the same language and traditions

potlatch—a feast with ceremonies and gifts among First Peoples of Canada

symbol—something that stands for something else. People use symbols to show what is important to them.

thunderbird—a mythical bird among First Peoples

totem—an image of something that is a symbol for a clan or other group

Read More

Gleason, Carrie. *British Columbia* (Canada Close Up). Markham, ON: Scholastic Canada, 2009.

McDermott, Gerald. *Raven: A Trickster Tale from the Pacific Northwest*. Boston, MA: Houghton Mifflin Harcourt, 2001.

Internet Sites

FactHound offers a safe, fun way to find Internet sites related to this book. All of the sites on FactHound have been researched by our staff.

Here's all you do:

Visit *www.facthound.com*

Type in this code: 9781491470923

 Check out projects, games and lots more at **www.capstonekids.com**

Index

Word Count: 286
Grade: 1
Early-Intervention Level: 17